Tea F

India Williams

Tea For Me © 2022 India Williams

All rights reserved.

No part of this publication may be reproduced, stored in a retrieval system, or transmitted, in any form or by any means, electronic, mechanical, photocopying, recording or otherwise, without the prior written permission of the presenters.

India Williams asserts the moral right to be identified as author of this work.

Presentation by *BookLeaf Publishing*

Web: www.bookleafpub.com

E-mail: info@bookleafpub.com

ISBN: 9789357214476

First edition 2022

Marion, Zoe and Nadine, for putting up with and believing in me.

ACKNOWLEDGEMENT

Book Leaf Publishing for a very weird but interesting opportunity.

PREFACE

If you don't like feminisim, anxiety or rhyming...just don't read it?

Hot Chocolate

Hands tremble as they
Circle the cup,
Praying the drink is
Worth the worry. The
Steam rises, swirling
Up, up, into the air. Breathe
It in - 1, 2, 3, 4.
Hold it, pause, for more.
Five. Then slow and
Sure, let the breath out.
7, 6, 5, repeat. Again.
Once was not enough. Once
Will never be enough.
In through the nose. Out
Through the mouth. Do
You feel better? Your
Hands may fall but no
Cup will break. It will
Be okay. You'll be just
Fine.

The Witch in the Woods

She lives in the woods,
With the tuneful forest birds.
She covets her crystals,
She harvests her herbs.

The woman with golden hair,
Piled on top of her head.
With snowdrop skin,
And eyes of hollyhock red.

She knows of her legend,
And the stories that are told:
Of a wretched scarred face,
And a heart, forever cold.

She teaches of nature:
About the animals and plants to please.
How to care for each and every creature,
Especially the spiders, and the bees.

She sings sweet lullabies,
And tells tales of magic from ancient days.
The witch in the wood,
A miracle upon which to gaze.

Christmas Tree

Twenty-three years old,
Covered in our memories,
Mis-matched and cosy.

Downtown

People run across the road
As rain comes lashing down.
A mother with a pushchair,
And her baby with a frown.

An umbrella open up above
Really? In this thunderstorm?
Sheltering with the ones you love;
The air outside still warm.

All colour seemingly drained,
Just the bright, red traffic light.
A moment still in motion,
On a crosswalk glistening bright.

What is this feeling?

What is this feeling
I have down deep inside?
What is this feeling
That makes me want to hide?
Oh, of course! I know what it is,
I've heard it said before.
In the words of Bo Burnham
"I feel like shit!"
Yeah, you'll find me on the floor.

You.

For two years you had me;
I was there under your nose.
We were friends through it all,
But you knew I wanted more.

When you put your hand on my leg,
When you give me that smile.
But was it all in my head?
When you charmed your way in?

You showed you were unreliable;
So mercilessly flaky.
You filled me up with hope,
But I was naïve enough to take it.

It took a while to get over.
You left me with an ache.
Now I'm glad nothing happened;
It would have ended in heartbreak.

We Are.

We are beauty,
We are strength,
We are pain,
We are hell bent,

On ensuring that
You don't fuck with us
Again.

Be an ally,
Be a friend,
Be a lover,
But not another,

One who won't hear 'no'
Or thinks they can control
Or try to give us less
Or continues to oppress.

We are fighting,
We are thriving,
We won't stand
For the conniving

Bastards who continually

Mistaken our struggle
For emotional and
Misguided aggression.

We are.

First Kiss

Part of a girls game;
About three on my short list.
I just wanted him.

Nice Guy Rebuttal

You do not own her,
She is not yours.
Her body, her choice.
She doesn't care what you prefer.

She is not a performer.
She is not an object.
Don't tell her to smile.
What did you expect?

What she is is beauty,
What she is is grace.
You don't deserve to have her.
She doesn't want to see your face.

Sister.

I love my sister,
Even when she's far too loud.
I'm glad she's around.

Regress.

Kids shows and movies -
They're an escape from this world.
Adult life is hard.

Smile

Smile to hide the pain.
Smile to hide the sadness.
Smile when asked "are you alright?"
The easiest of answers.
Smile for your joy.
Smile for a greeting.
Smile before they notice
You've gone hours without eating.
Smile for the breakthroughs.
Smile each time you speak.
Smile because she's there for you -
It does not make you weak.

Words of Comfort

You are brave,
You are smart,
You are beautiful,
You are kind.
I don't know you,
You don't know me;
But I'm out there
Believing in you,
Saying you have worth.
There are people
In this world
Who love you as you are.
They know you have purpose,
You should believe it too.
I know what you think:
"No one understands"
"I don't want to feel like this"
"It feels like it won't end"
"I'll never be normal again"
"It's always there lurking,
A shadow on my back"
I want you to know,
It will get bearable.
You can survive,
Just keep going,

You will get through.
One step at a time,
That's all you need to do.

Colour-coded

Rose pink is for calming,
Deep red is Christmas joy,
Bright yellow is happy sunshine,
Lilac I do enjoy.

Pale blue is for the clearest sky,
Emerald green is mother earth,
Pure white is the first blank page,
Darkest black is Wednesday's shirt.

Feminism!

Feminism is
Great. We want equality.
Huh, that's funny,
You say you don't?
Then be our enemy.

To all my friends...

To all my frIends out thEre;
You kNow juSt who you Are.
Some of you Live nearby,
Some of you Are far.

I'm beyond lucky to have you;
The very best people I know.
I'm shItty at keepinG in touch with you,
So I would just like you to know...

I appreciate the years,
Or even just the Months,
You've bEen puttIng up with me,
And all my (mental) lumps and bumps.

Don't know what I'd do without you,
I truly love you all.
I'm grateful to have met you,
I'll always pick up every text and call.

MGG

Shoulder-length, chocolate coloured, wavy hair.

Eyes of the same hue with a child-like glint.

A mouth that's wide in a perfect, warm grin.

Manicured stubble, highlighting the chin.

A man so sweet and humble, talented

And generous, and he never ages.

With a goofy disposition - charming,

And creative. God made men then gave us

Him as a big apology.

That Boston friend of mine

She's funny and she's
kind. Supportive and sarcastic.
The best damn co I
Could have had. That Boston friend
Of mine.

I taught her English
Phrases. She taught me how to
Survive. I like how
She says water. That
Boston friend of mine.

For three months we lived
Together. Sometimes with a
Mouse. I miss her and
Her hugs. That Boston friend of
Mine.

Just by being you

I haven't known you long,
You don't know me at all,
But you've changed my life
Forever. Just by being you.
You've helped me overcome,
My struggles and my pain.
You always make me happy,
Just by being you.
Thank you for the music,
Thank you for the stages.
Thank you for the magic you made,
Just by being you.
You've done so much good
For this world and everyone in it.
Sometimes you don't even know,
Which shows your humility,
Your kindness and your courage,
Your talent, your endurance,
Your beauty and your honesty.
Seven purple hearts that will
Never be forgotten. The purest
Souls on the earth we will
Never take for granted.
Some say it sounds dramatic,
Some say that it sounds silly,

To love people you've never met.
But we know you love us too.
You brought us into your family,
Together you're our home.
We'll love you 'till the end of days.
You've brightened up our lives,
Just by being by our side,
Just by being you.

Me.

I don't know what I am
Or where I'm s'posed to be.
I'm doing what I can
To be okay with me.

A list of simple things

Hot chocolate and cake baking,
Vanilla and gingerbread.
Cosy, fluffy blankets,
A bucket hat on my head.
Colourful, comfy jumpers,
Books and Arts and Crafts.
Austen down to Mercer,
Films that make me laugh.
Dancing, writing, yoga,
Dan and Phil and Taylor Swift.
BTS above all else,
That's how my mood can lift.